EPIC

JOY · WISDOM · PAIN

BY GINN WILLIAMS
PHOTOGRAPHY BY IAN YOUNG

EIGHTY·SEVEN·AND·NINE

Copyright © 2008 by Ginn Williams

All rights reserved. No part of this book may be reproduced or utilized in an form or by any means, electronic or mechanical, including photocopying, recording, or by any information storage or retrieval system, without permission in writing from the Publisher.

Library of Congress Cataloging-in-Publication Data
Epic
Ginn Williams (Poet)
Ian Young (Photographer)

ISBN 978-0-6151-9257-4

Printed in the United States of America
First Edition

DEDICATED TO

IAN

JENRAVEN

&

MY FATHER

CHAPTER ONE
LOVE

Love Being in Love
Bakersfield, Ca

In You

I want to love you like life,
deeply, intensely, and fully.
Push myself inside of you,
feeling you, absorbing you.
Imprinting your image in my mind,
Inviting your soul into my heart,
Leaving my kisses inside and all around you.
Float along the surface of your thoughts
Letting your fantasies cling to me,
Glistening on my skin.
Up to my elbows in the essence that is you,
Run my fingers around the edges.
Rub you between my palms,
Letting you drip from my fingers.
Tasting the warmth,
Around the ankles,
Up the thigh,
Rounding at the waist
But leaving off at the lips.
Touch your heart,
Dwell in your thoughts,
And gently kiss your soul.
I want to love you like life,
deeply, intensely,
and fully.

The Admirer
Los Angeles, CA

16 BARS

If I was both his blessing and his best friend
Would he still fear something as foolish as the end?
Life begins with that last breath
Fearing the non-existent.
What we call death
He laid down 16 bars
16 bars to that dark angelic chord in my heart
16 bars back to the start
Where we first intertwined
And he redefined
What it meant to be encased among angels and demons
Finding myself playing it safe for the obvious reasons
And just when I thought the suffer was finished,
In steps the smallest piece of the puzzle
The one that makes that picture click.
My memory tick
And my mind spill forth that spiritual pain
Just for two more breaths gained
Just to be with him
I can't determine if loving you has blocked my destiny
or fulfilled it
Because love is sometimes like my shoes don't know
till you've walked in it
In his eyes is the memory of each lifetime we met
In each one by his side I was set
Can't seem to pay off our history of spiritual debt
But infected by sin just how far can we get
He reasons with his demons instead of casting them out
Can't imagine what can be achieved on a different route
As large black wings stretch from my spine
They seem to overshadow is slanted halo and bring him
close to call him mine
As other ones whisper to him softly everything is fine
He won't believe and still can't see
he comes from the Divine
And when he finds me praying to God and pleading
with the devil in my sleep
Negotiation is out the window
and the price isn't cheap
Just to spare what I see left in him
The best in him
He has no idea who he is
Always on the defensive
Takes me as dismissive
Can't help when his tone is derisive
Shrinking my being into submissive
My bipolar, ADD, sweet Steel Reserve covered high
Drowning me deep in a thick heated liquid low
Mixed, poured, shaped, condensed and compact.
Perfectly preserved and candy coated.
Mass produced for your personal pleasure
but never promoted
Still feel like I can't obtain him
Although he says I contain him
I feel I only sustain him
And though I try, still can't explain him
If only 10 minutes to feel what I feel
10 minutes to carry a wound that won't heal
10 minutes in the dark reaching for a hand
10 minutes just for 1 minute to understand
He is my love, my gift, my courage and might
My pain, my suffer, my burden, my light
Can't remember time before him,
before he made it right
Through all that's good and bad he'll fight
And as life turns pages I'll continue to write
A chronicle to place in heaven in angels' sight
And when we meet again
at the house of the Divine
You close your eyes and I'll close mine
We'll find ourselves back in this lifetime
Past mistakes we'll both transcend
And one more time I'll ask again
If I am your blessing and your best friend
Would you still fear something
as foolish as the end?

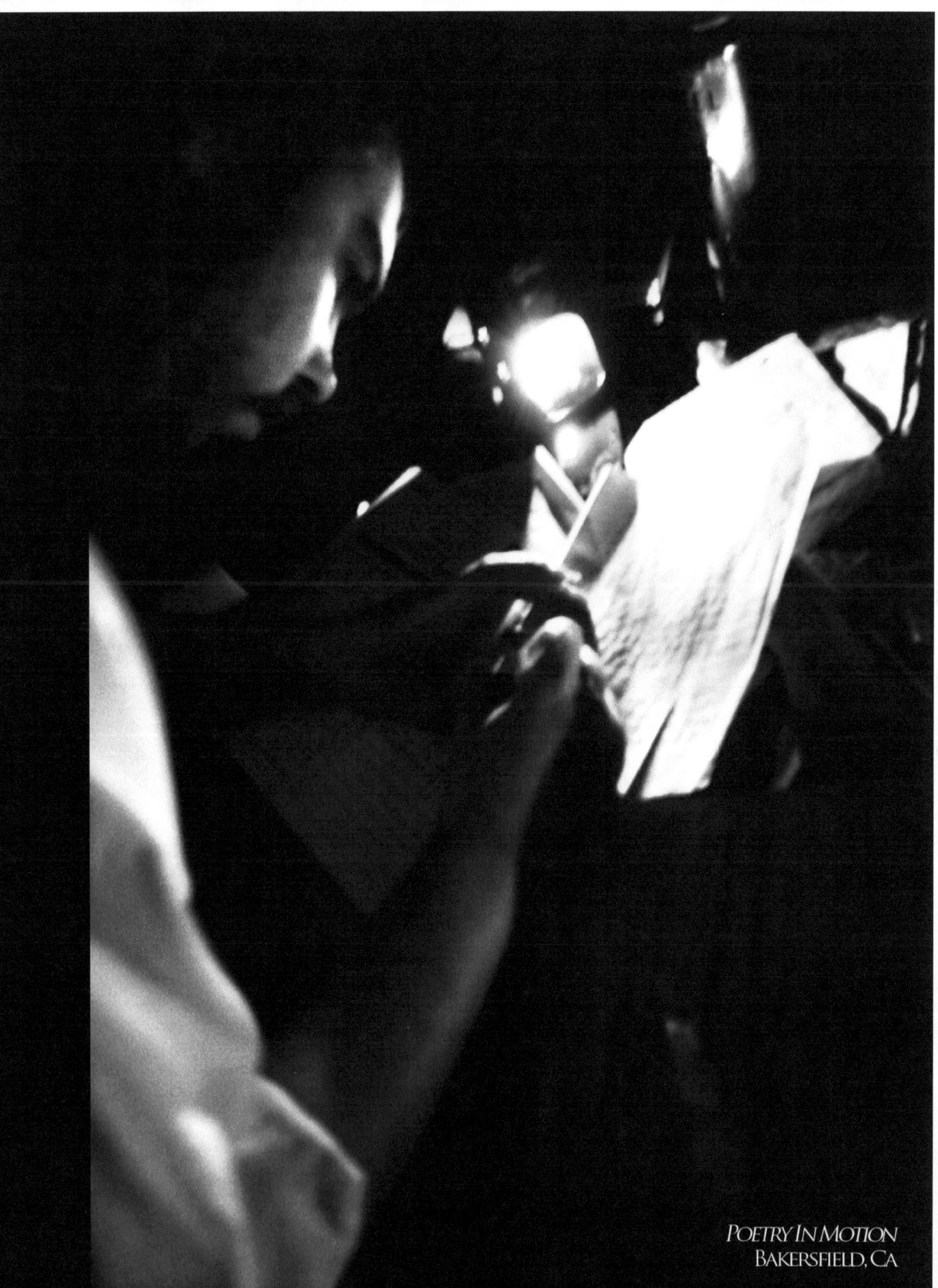

Poetry In Motion
Bakersfield, Ca

THE FIGURES

35,942,400 Seconds
599,040 Minutes
9,984 Hours
416 Days
410 Miles
358 Phone Calls
149 Dollars
56 Pieces of Paper
39 Nights
17 Heartfelt Cries
13 Months
8 Attempts to make it work
5 Minutes writing this,
and
2 I Love You's
Wasted, on you

The Price of a Broken Heart is Costly
Bakersfield, CA

DONT TELL ME

Don't tell me you're a man
Tell me you're
Morally challenged
Intellectually insufficient
A disrespectful
Disoriented
Delusional
Conscience absent
Certified
Space cadet
Tell me you're
Emotionally bankrupt
Ultra alcoholic
Marijuana junkie
Insecure
Incompetent
Professional complainer
A perfectly pessimistic
Problem maker
Impassionate
And
Verbally offensive
Tell me you're
Immature
A breast lovin'
Booty watchin'
In your face
Late night
Masturbating to Cinemax perv
A financially dependent
Beer guzzling
Football fanatic
On the fast track to no where
But don't tell me you're a man

CHAPTER TWO
HURT

Michael
Bakersfield, Ca

The Forecast

I can feel the distance stretching out between us,
A situation so blind based on pure similarity and sensory.
In some moments sensing the captivation fading
Becoming blunt and bored on your part
Hearing the egg shells crack beneath my feet.
You find contradiction
In the justification of my physical engagements that starve my mind,
The result, a mal nourished heart.
Yet by the same token you appear to find solace
In my mental and emotional fascination with you,
Almost as if playing a strategic mind game of chess
Blaming each checkmate on the alignment of the stars
under which you were born.
I dig you but I can't obtain you
I feel you but I can't conceive you
You spark my curiosity but I can't get to know you
Your capacity for understanding is overwhelming but
I need to be viewed for more than typical.

The Look of Love
Bakersfield, Ca

ABOUT YESTERDAY

I'm sorry I didn't come to see you yesterday
I'm sorry I haven't spent more time knowing who you are
Just last week my dad said
"You don't know how to play dominoes?
Man your uncle's so good he can tell you what's in
your hand and what you better play." At that time I
thought what a good idea,
I'll have to go over sometime and pick up some more skills
I wonder what it would be like if
I thought like that about my dad
Sounds great I'll have to go visit one day

I'm sorry I didn't come see you yesterday
There are clips and pictures
Of birthday parties and of grandma's house with you in them
None just you and me
And yet I couldn't take it to make yesterday that day
Of you and me
Once is too many times to be put in a small room
And have what life comes down to explained to you
I can't take the look of it
The smell of it
The cold touch to it

I'm sorry I didn't come to see you yesterday
The day I realized that when they took your breath away
And watched them shut down one by one
Just as they did twice before you
My father stands somewhere in line behind you
And yet it's not you I feel bad for it's him
Because you have a piece I don't have
Because what you are now I am happy for you
Because I understand the beginning
And I envy that you got to go

I'm sorry I didn't come to see you yesterday
The last day you were alive.

E-V-I-L
(LIVE)

I don't blame him for turning his back to me
It's nothing but the live in me
E-V-I-L
So deeply rooted only he and I can tell
The repetition in emotional hell
I shouted till I thought God could no longer hear me
Be near me
Shaken out every tear
Beat out of me the fear
Build me to break me
Make me to forsake me
She said it's what you can bear
But what can I spare
When the tragedy of it is me
Too uncomfortable to simply be
And the tapestry of my life tends to cling
Till what I carry inside starts to sting
When all that's between us is that distance,
For instance
Distance of word to word or page to page
If I've enlisted rage then let me gauge
The intensity of the present stage
I just want to perform a piece of mine
Reform a broken mind
So where do we stand
In the midst of command
Or the depths of demand
But in the deduction
What's reached is destruction
In the construction of pain
Without even loss of self to gain

Stand-Up Guy

I knew he wasn't shit from the jump.
I knew he wasn't shit when his momma sat me down and said,
"Girl, he's a ho and a liar just like his daddy!"
When your kids are 45 days apart and you have to have
custody of one of them
Because the baby mama is less than your ain't shit ass.
Now you say you're turnin' in your player card cause
you gave someone a ring.
That's like a crack head turnin' in his pipe
Because his dental plan don't cover crack related condtions.
We've tried this one before
Only the burn wasn't in your draws when you found her
in your bed with the next man.
You got off lucky considering you were ho'in it up too.
Married women, ugly women, broke women, taken women,
It's all the same in the dark to you.
So why should I view you any different.
So don't look me in the face like you're a stand up guy
When the dent in your mattress says otherwise.
You ain't shit!

A Predator and His Prey
Bakersfield, Ca

CHAPTER THREE
LIFE

The Shepard
Bakersfield, Ca

CONTROL ISSUE

Much like the way a single grain of sand on some level
Displaces the whole ocean.
There are billions of things that can affect our being,
Billions of situations, people, events,
And worldly things to keep a firm grip to,
Billions of things that can displace our entire being.
Affecting the entire picture viewed through
kaleidoscope eyes,
Different at every angle.
Altered from the physical to the chemical concoction
that spins us drunk
Creating a serum of panic that lines the chest,
Not painful but always noticeably present.
Before you know it
You find yourself waiting for the next grain of sand
to shift your being
Back into what you thought was its own self sufficient force.
Delegating each position aware of each moment,
In reality still a product of the one
Who even when things are carried by our hands
Moves our emotions directing the feet to the correct place.
On some levels anxiety is a blessing
Its presence brings you aware to what is no longer in your control
Although its absence brings us back to the dream that it is.

Curiosity Got The Best Of Me
Bakersfield, CA

SUICIDE

I tried to commit suicide this week,
thought about it for two whole days.
Most would say if I'm serious just get to the point however,
Indecisiveness caused me to procrastinate.
See I seem to have this imaginary disease
That keeps me in bed for days at a time
Causes me to break into tears for no reason.
A disease that is all in my head and I have complete control over.
I tried to commit suicide this week
But I couldn't decide between my clozapine pills or a razor to my wrist.
I woke up to 2007 thinking
Do I really want to spend another year being already psychologically deceased?
What do I really have,
Loved ones that can't comprehend,
My illusion of picture perfect health or
How about my possessions,
My many possessions that carry no sentiment.
So selfish is the person that lives for themselves,
Even more selfish are those who wish you to continue living for them.
So if I could rip this disease from me,
Hold it out in my hands for you to see the pain,
Would it still be so imaginary?
Does my ability to breathe give me the ability to as you say snap out of it?
Should I just all the sudden start thanking God
That I don't have it as hard as the next person?
After all I haven't lost all my earthly possessions,
just myself.
So should I hide my face and feel ashamed
That I don't ask God for money or fame or worldly things.
Just to do for me what I procrastinate to do
Not out of uncertainty but exhaustion.
Maybe you have a magical cure for this imaginary disease
That lines my insides and clogs my soul.
So a better posed question,
Different perspective.
Let's say you believed and knew it was real.
Can you call me suicidal or terminally ill?
And if death was the only cure
Can you really blame me for going to the extreme
to live again?

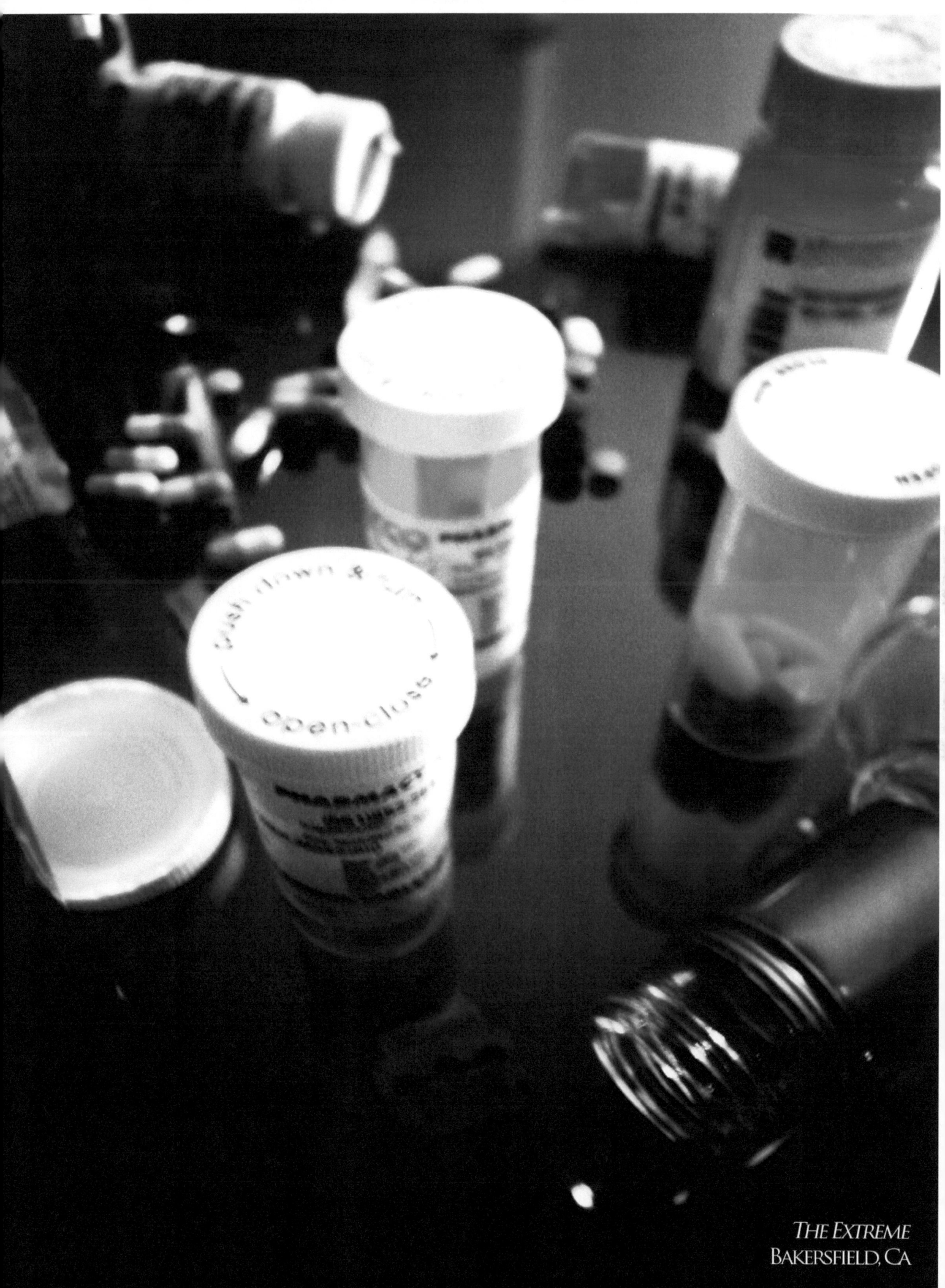

TRACK #3

To rise and brim,
The decision to yield or overflow.
To sink down in a rich familiar or
Reach out into deep desire.
Wanting to achieve the future dreams of two as one
And the need to correct a spiritual connection of love gone by.
A fire in the unconscious burning a hole in reality
Sparking the physical to attain a mental peace
Among melodies and memories
Faces of inspiration, wisdom,
Bonds deeper and stronger than genetics,
Beauty beyond a visual level,
And love that transcends this lifetime.
I choose to overflow,
Over the past, the pain, the loves, the losses, time
wasted, and time spent.
Overflow in content with the present,
In the beauty, joy, warmth, mystery, and love that is my own.
Sometimes, to hold on, you have to let go,
Find comfort in the certainty of a transition,
Have peace with what is gone,
And a belief of finding one another again
through the Divine.

Decisions
Bakersfield, Ca

EPIC

I am a hero,
King of sorrow,
Creator of joy,
Master of the universe,
And the author of my horoscope.
In my mind.
One look from me and inspiration busts at the seams,
Magic in my pocket as I pull your strings
for my masterpieces.
Yet inside,
Where it's uneasy and unsure yet more comfortable than
my favorite shoes.
I don't want you to see who I am;
I don't want you to know my needs, desires, acts,
or thoughts.
Myself my only counsel, myself my only confidante,
myself my only hurdle.
I don't want you to see how she broke my heart;
I don't want you to see how uncomfortable people are
with open eyes and open mouths,
Outside of still life.
I don't want you to see the thoughts of suicide,
The depression, and the fear of shining,
Not wanting to attract attention to myself.
But in my efforts to keep you blind,
You may miss my ability to make you see what you could
not without my lens.
The eccentricity of every twist and turn of my mind,
How relaxed and inviting I can be
With just the touch of my hand on your shoulder.
How I can tell your stories without saying a word
And capture everyone's light making my own
impossible to completely hide.
I am a hero,
King of sorrow,
Creator of joy,
Master of the universe,
And the author of my horoscope.
In my mind.

Valiant Humility
Los Angeles, Ca

CHAPTER FOUR
MOVING ON

Leaving Lafrac, NY

AFFLICTION

Life at times can feel like just a complication of death
Finding myself praying to be simple,
Wanting so badly to lower my frequency to that level of ignorance
So blissfully enjoyed by those who are not the Processors and interpreters of this affliction called human.
The disrespect in dissection of grief
Brought by those who only nod and hear never being able to feel and listen
I can't vibe without you, feeling inferior each time I vibe with you
Yet amazed each time my vibe grows within you.
My kindred vessels being chosen for a path of trials and tribulation
With no certainty of reward.
Having only each other to invest in
Considered too intellectual.
Outcast yet casting out the mediocrity of it all
As industries come forth with slanted halos
Perched over pointed horns.
Bearing death in fortune through promises of that anonymous persona destroyed.
The chance for your pieces of overstanding to seep unto those incapable,
All the while they ride the backs of the Divines messengers
To that false promise land they've created for even themselves
To never see anything but the big picture
Yet aware of every detail.
Dignified with responses of focus,
Intertwined visions of self.

There are those moments when it never got this good.
Never felt this good.
When your soul cries for that roar just one more time.
To step up on high and have it surrounds you.
Amplified.
Holding onto that mic just as tightly as to who you thought yourself to be.
There are those of us that do this just for the compensation.
Prostitution of art.
There are those of us who spill forth their talent
So much so to the point of wasteful.
Purely for the will to do so.
Then there are those of us who have no choice,
Do this because they must breath.
It beckons us, and destroys us, and builds us.
Imprisons us, and cripples us yet frees us, makes us,
At times being the only one that loves us.
It conceived me and consumed me;
It related me then changed me.
Finding myself envious of those who don't walk day to day with truth
Sitting in their back pocket
Biting you in the ass each time you sit among those Who aren't enslaved to that pen and pad,
That constant stirring in your mind
That wakes you to that cold reality in A.M. hours.
All behind this,
A single sentence.

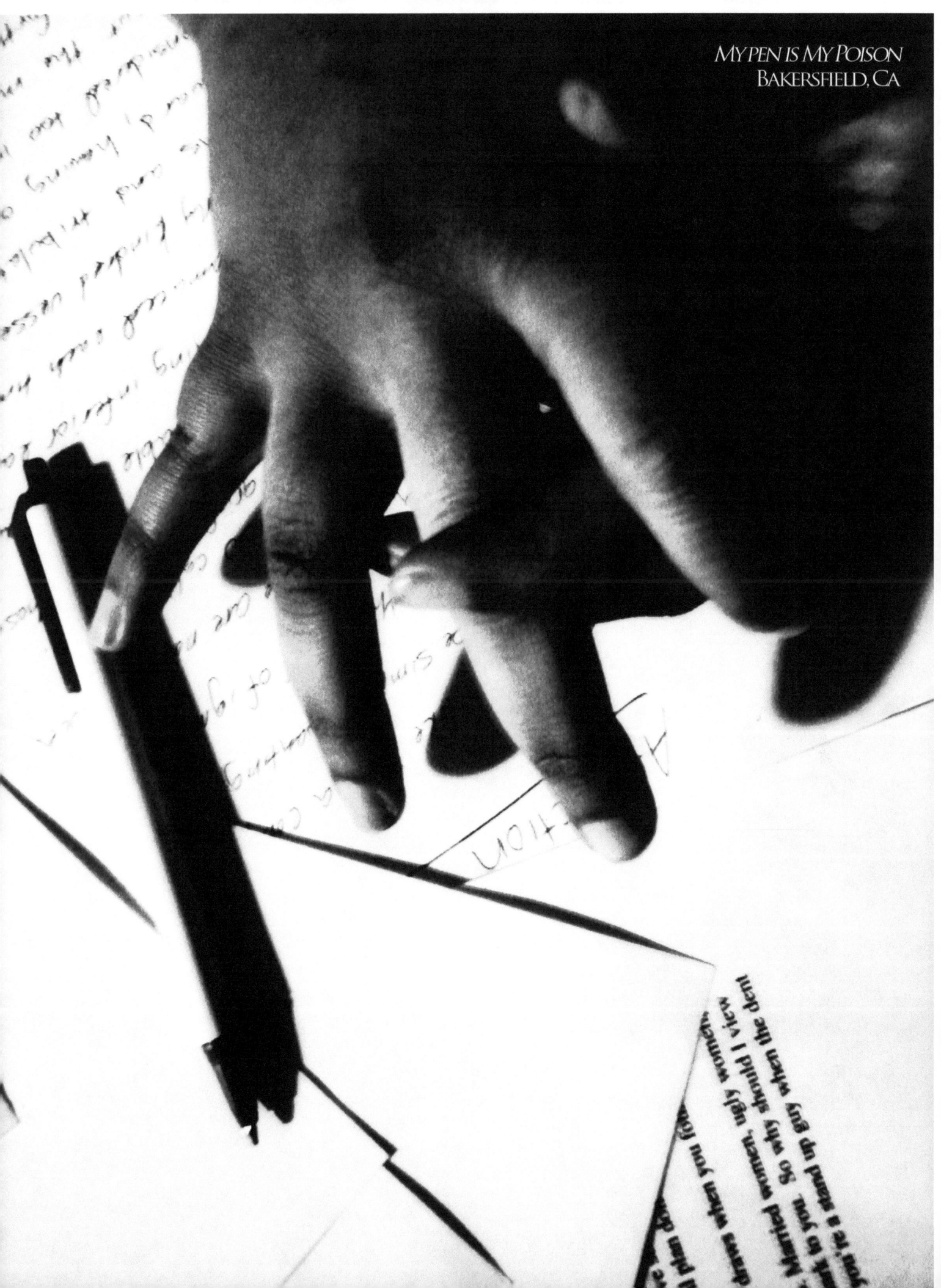

My Pen Is My Poison
Bakersfield, CA

Universal Liquid

If every face had no name,
Every word had no meaning,
And every emotion was empty.
Would you know me, hear me, or even feel me.
If we all walked the same path to an open space
Would there be enough room,
Like stars in a sky we all shine but who decides who shines brightest.
What is it that moves our souls encased in insignificant masses,
We carry this thing called faith that's placed in different things
All higher than us,
An energy implanted in our center
Causing noise to spill out of the mouth
Some attaching to another some falling to the ground
And being evaporated into the atmosphere causing pollution,
Making it hard for the eyes to see through
Creating chaos while we bump heads and struggle.
We fill our minds with knowledge for paper,
Not thinking about the wisdom we need to consume to survive,
All the while striving to be such emotionless beings
Yet the fire can be placed in our bellies so easily
Making us fight with the need to be similar yet different at the same time,
Traveling down the same path but getting lost in the crowd
Searching for different planes in other dimensions that may not exist.
The only thing moving our physical chamber is the confusion
About when life ends and when it begins,
Whether it's the first breath or the last,
Feeling spiritually ignorant under a blanket of worldly information.

The Drink
Queens, NY

MY ART

I am not come to call the inclined
But those who are incapable to the suffer
For I so loved those who know not
I gave my only begotten affliction
My addiction
My passion
My strive
My drive
My all, my
Life
Dedicated
Reiterated
Tolerated
So loved yet hated
Belated
Life
My art
No restitution
In prostitution
No substitution
No absolution
Yet no solution
In this institution
Called Art
My art
Consumes me
Yet assumes me
At times can
Presume me
As it resumes me
My Art

A Moment's Peace
Long Beach, Ca

I AM

I am
I am invincible
Timeless
I am worthy
An explosion outside the box
I am a philosopher in a nation with no philosophy
A new mind among old concepts
I am what happens when life happens
I am a white wave
A black star
A red flame
And as green as the cash in your pocket
I am my own best friend
My first true love
I am my favorite poet
I am Alpha and Omega
I am you
I am me
I am

CHAPTER FIVE
OH SHIT!

You's A Fat Bitch

You's a fat bitch!
She said as I walked on by
Supporting her meth-head frame
on a pair of toothpicks
she called stilettos.
With her barely there titties and an
ass so flat you
can evenly hang a picture on it.
You's a fat bitch!
She said as I walked on by
Bottled water in hand, with her
trim yet un-toned body
Implants displaying her cheapness
from the sports bra
Face done up like a Picasso!
And that towel to catch the
pretend sweat that she
sweats on that stair master.
Using all her brain power to
distinguish the lawyers
and doctors from the scrubs
Without the visual aid of a briefcase
or a stethoscope.
You's a fat bitch!
Why!?
Because my thighs rub when I walk?
Does the swoosh sound they make
disturb you?
Is it because my stomach hangs
below my beltline?
Would it be more visually appealing
if I gave a fuck
how long my shirt is?
Maybe it's the cankles, is it the
cankles?
No, I don't think socks will help.
I know!
It's the dimples in my ass!
No?
The way my titties sag because
they're large?
No I don't think your Victoria's
Secret bra will fix that.
I need a little more that two band
aids and a fishing line.
How about the way my arms can wave
goodbye in two places?
No?
Well shit!
Maybe I'm a fat bitch because I can be!
Because there's more to life than the
size of your draws.
Because what's important is what
comes out your mouth
Not what you put in it
(I'm not talking about the ho's,
ho's excluded, ya'll bitches is nasty!)
Because if I want to sit on my fat ass
and hold an intelligent
conversation with someone
or stand on my cankles and spit
some real shit for real people
with more than two
brain cells to rub together,
Guess what,
I will!
If I want to eat meat like
God intended
and have chocolate cake
instead of a bullshit ass
glass of water,
Guess what,
I will!
I'm not gonna bust my heart open
on the treadmill
because your vision is fucked up!
And if you're mad, get over it!
God just loves me more,
He only gave you one chin.

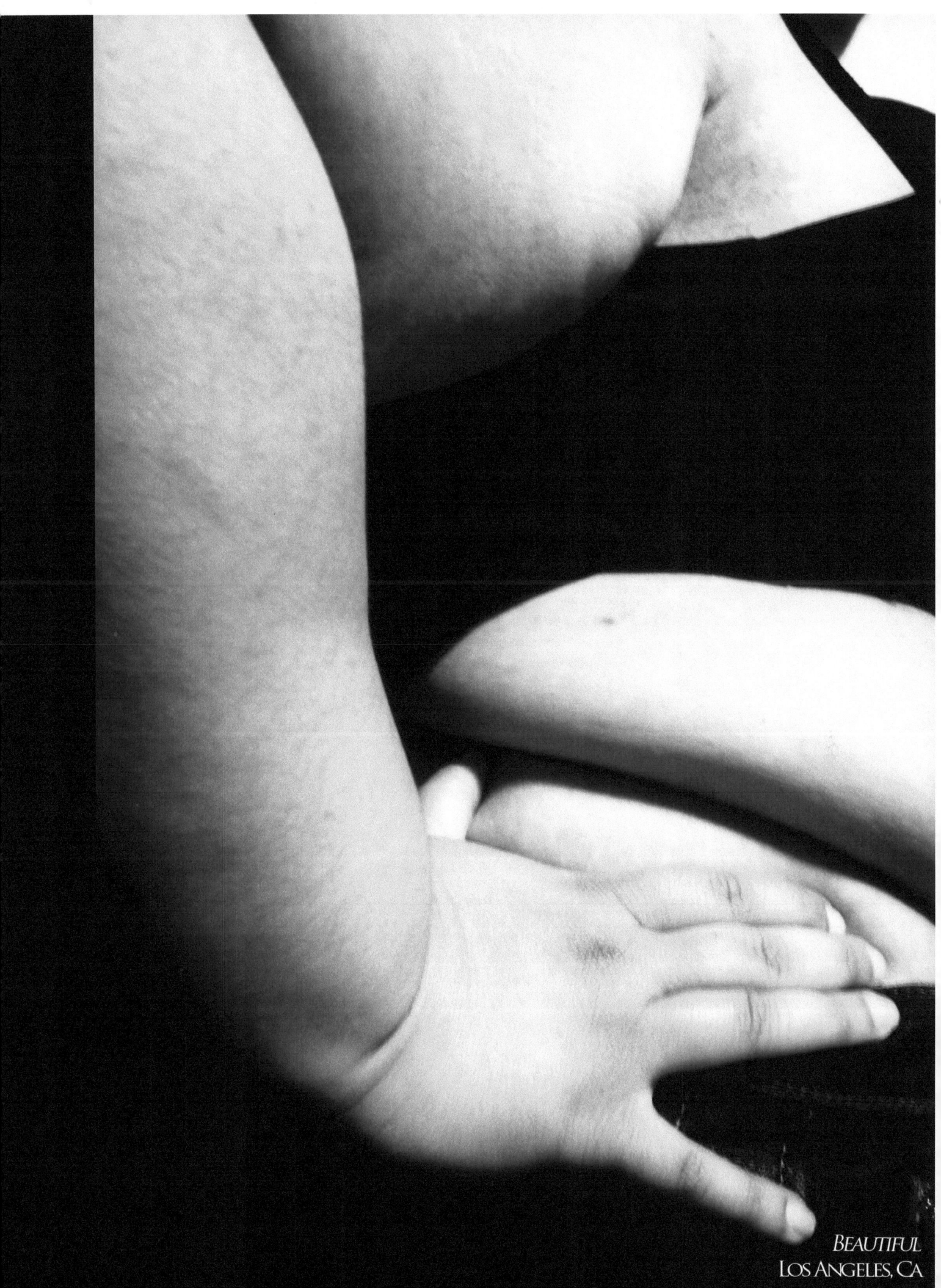

Beautiful
Los Angeles, CA

Dayum Did You Feel That?

Took me for a disgruntle bitch,
said my tongue was like a double
edged sword
Said I cut your self-esteem up,
mentally bankrupt,
well let me spit something you
can afford
Thought I was finished, thought
I'd lay low
Dayum I was right your grind
ain't the only thing
that's slow
And speakin' of slow apply it to
your roll
Fuck around and find yourself
suckin' on some emotional pole
Men don't get it twisted them
broads got it comin' too
Thought you got out of it, bitch
set your ass down
I ain't through
Your salty presence has got my
blood pressure on the rise
Mad cause he found out second
best was in between your thighs
Man fuck an irritation,
I'm pissed the fuck off
Just because there's no
confrontation
Don't take me for soft
We were thick as thieves when
your hands were in my
pockets stacked with cash
Now you act like I ain't shit,
broke my back reaching
round for my last
There is no such thing as a
female friend,
only shady bitches you know and
backstabbing broads you hate
Gave you a whole fuckin' pie but
you steadily bitchin'
bout the last piece of cake
A way to put you in your place,
conceived it
The destruction of your being,
achieved it
The sweet taste of revenge,
received it
Infest you to the molecules with
realism, believe it
See I'm an equal opportunity
female when it comes to
shootin' out my anger
Better strap on your bulletproof
cause your feelings
are in danger
Did you really think it affected
me that attitude you cop
You roll your eyes one more time
and that ego I'll pop
Go ahead and test my mouthpiece
but I'm telling you now
it's like fire
What I want is beyond this world
and what I need
you can't acquire
So you can sleep in the dream of
your stature and
drown deep in denial
What?
You say you're how tall?
Dayum I didn't know shit came in
that big of a pile.

FURY OF THE SCORNED
BAKERSFIELD, CA

I WANNA BE A DEF POET

THE PAST FEW YEARS ALL I CAN THINK IS
I WANNA BE A DEF POET
RUSSELL SIMMONS, MOS DEF,
COMMON, TALIB KWALI
INNOVATORS OF AN ENTIRE CULTURE,
LEGENDS TO ME
WITH ALL THE MIGHT
AND WISDOM GIVEN TO THEE
I'LL PART THEIR MINDS AND INHIBITIONS AS
THE RED SEA
TAKE YOUR IMAGINATION ON A THOUGHT
PROVOKING SPENDING SPREE
EMOTIONAL ROLLER COASTER OF
REVELATIONS TO THE THIRD DEGREE
AS I PUT UPON STORIES OF LOVE,
SACRIFICE AND BEAUTY IN ONE DECREE
THE LEGACY OF MY HEART I WILL
GUARANTEE
AND ALL THAT HEAR IT CANT DISAGREE
AS I LET LOSE AND SHARE MY ONLY PLEA
HERE WE GO 1,2,3
WHEN I WRITE DON'T KNOW WHERE IT'S
GONNA LEAD
WHAT MIND IT'S GONNA FEED
SEE THROUGH THE BULL
FIND YOUR BELLIES FULL
BECAUSE IN THIS WORLD THERE'S NO
JUSTICE
THERE'S JUST US
SO LET ME JUST TAKE IT SLOW
AND LET IT GROW
LET MY ENVIOUS SPIRIT
REACH THAT PLATEAU
WELCOME TO THE SHOW

I WANNA BE A DEF POET
REIGNING DOWN ON MY SUBJECTS
AS IF I WAS QUEEN
WHERE ITS ALL OR NOTHING
NO IN BETWEEN
MONDAY NIGHTS
PUT TOGETHER SOMETHING HOT
WEDNESDAY NIGHTS
I WANNA LET IT ROCK
WITH MY INTERPRETATION
MY EMANCIPATION
FROM WHAT IS ME
I'VE SETTLED FOR THAT DUST BOWL
THAT FEELS LIKE A FISH BOWL
LONG FOR THAT SMALL POND WITH A
MILLION FISH
MY ONLY WISH

I WANNA BE A DEF POET
BRING DOWN BARRIERS
LIKE SAUL WILLIAMS
SPEAK ON BLACK SLAVES AND PILGRIMS
IN PRESENT DAY CHAINS
FRONTIERS OF TECHNOLOGY
MEDIAS RANGE
WHERE OUTLAWS WEAR BLING
AND OUR PEOPLE HAVE
FORGOTTEN TO SING
FREE AT LAST, FREE AT LAST, THANK GOD
ALMIGHTY FREE AT LAST
MOST YOUNG PEOPLE HAVEN'T FELT
A FIRE HOSE BLAST
HOW EASILY THEY FORGET
HISTORY ISN'T NECESSARILY THE PAST
JUST A SIDE OF THE STORY TOLD BY THOSE
THAT SURPASSED

AND ALTHOUGH I'VE NOT ENCOUNTERED
DOG BITES AND POLICEMAN BATS
MY FATHER'S BIRTH CERTIFICATE IS STILL
LABELED COLORED,
ADDRESSED TEXAS FLATS

I WANNA BE A DEF POET
I WANT TO SPEAK ON
HOW AS AN AMER-I-CAN
I CAN
BE HOMELESS AND IN THE STREETS
BE A FILLER FOR EMPTY SEATS
DIE OF SOMETHING FROM
NO MEDICAL CARE
YET FOR ILLEGALS TO BE WELL AND
UNREPORTED,
I PAY THE FARE
WHERE I CAN'T WORK BECAUSE I DON'T
SPEAK THE LANGUAGE
OF A COUNTRY I'M NOT FROM
WHERE THE GOVERNMENT SUGARCOATS
FREE LABOR AND EXPECTS
US TO PLAY DUMB
AS AN AMER-I-CAN
I CAN
BE EDITED
DISCREDITED
WATCH MY CHILDREN STARVE
MY ELDERS LOSE ALL THEY'VE CARVED
OUT OF THIS AMER-I-CAN
I CAN
DREAM

I WANNA BE A DEF POET
I WANT TO SPEAK ON ANGELS AND DEMONS
AND DON'T FORGET ALL THE RIGHT
REASONS
WHY WE LIVE THIS LIFE IN MEASUREMENTS
OF TIME WASTED AND TIME SPENT
GET YOUR MIND BENT
AND WRAPPED AROUND A DIFFERENT
CONCEPT
THEN LETS RECEPT
THE EXTREMELY UNKEMPT
MANNER IN WHICH
UNDER THE RUG IT WAS SWEPT
WHILE FATHER TIME CREPT
STEALING LIFE AS WE SLEPT
AND OH HOW WE WEPT
WHEN WE COULDN'T ACCEPT
OVER THAT BOUNDARY WED STEPPED
MY THINKING YOU MUST EXCUSE
WHEN I SAY THE WORLD NEEDS A MUSE
TO ONCE AGAIN LIGHT THE FUSE
DISREGARD THE SNOOZE
SHAKE THE BLUES
AND SEE "WE" AND "US" IN DIFFERENT VIEWS

I WANNA BE A DEF POET
WITH MY WORDS I'LL BUILD NATIONS
SEND OUT THE UNIVERSAL VIBRATIONS
TO REACH THE MOST REMOTE LOCATIONS
IMPROVING SPIRITUAL AND HUMAN
RELATIONS
THEN I'LL BECOME AS THOSE IDOLS AND
LEGENDS TO ME
THAT SEEK ME OUT EVERY WEEK ON MY TV
AND ALTHOUGH I'M NO EMCEE
I WAS DESTINED TO BE
ONE OF THE BEST YOU'LL SEE
ON DEF POETRY.

THE EULOGY

I only agreed to come today if I could
tell the truth
The truth is I didn't love
nor respect her
A twisted dark soul
if a soul ever existed
Will kick you when you're down
Spit in your face
And piss in your cornflakes
I could not respect a lie or a cheat
I could not love a heartless chamber
I could not care about
a cruel swindler
Tie breaker bridge burner
Manipulative to the toes
I didn't love nor respect her
However I thank her for being cold
as slabs of marble
For teaching me how to deal
with what the world could be
but shouldn't
For teaching me how
not to live my life
I didn't love
nor respect her
And that's all I can say
about my mom.

UnLoved
Bakersfield, Ca

www.ingramcontent.com/pod-product-compliance
Lightning Source LLC
Chambersburg PA
CBHW042010150426
43195CB00002B/80